HEDGEHOGS

THE ESSENTIAL GUIDE TO OWNERSHIP & CARE FOR YOUR PET

Kate H. Pellham

DISCLAIMER

Although the author and publisher have made every effort to ensure that the information in this book was correct at press time, the author and publisher do not assume and hereby disclaim any liability to any party for any loss, damage, or disruption caused by errors or omissions, whether such errors or omissions result from negligence, accident, or any other cause.

This book is not intended as a substitute for the medical advice of a veterinarian. The reader should regularly consult a veterinarian in matters relating to his/her pet's health and particularly with respect to any symptoms that may require diagnosis or medical attention.

Photos copyright respective owners, licensed through stock sites unless otherwise noted.

Table of Contents

Chapter 1: Introduction to Hedgehogs

Hedgehog is the common name for any one of approximately 14 species in the family *Erinaceidae* that live throughout Europe, Asia, and Africa, most distinctively recognized by their back full of quills. When threatened, hedgehogs will roll up into a ball with their quills raised, a defensive maneuver designed to ward off casual predators. Aside from the presence of quills, the physical attributes of hedgehogs vary widely between species. They can be as short as 5 inches long, or as long as 15. Their weight can range from 200-1000 grams, and their coloration can be anywhere from pure white to nearly black, with variants of browns, creams, and grays in between.

The range of hedgehogs is broad, stretching from Norway to South Africa and from Britain to China. They've even been introduced to New Zealand, though they're not a native species, meaning the only continents where you can't find wild hedgehogs are North and South America. While hedgehogs as a group cover three continents and a wide range of biomes, each individual hedgehog species has a more limited range. Some species live in the forests and fields of temperate regions and hibernate to survive the cold winters. Others are more accustomed to the hot, arid climate of North Africa, where their territory includes both desert and scrubland, and the hedgehog hides from the heat during the day, coming out at night to forage. Whatever the species, hedgehogs are opportunistic feeders. They're classified as insectivores but will eat pretty much anything that seems edible.

The most distinctive feature of a hedgehog is its quills. There are approximately 7,000 quills on an adult hedgehog's back. Scientifically speaking, quills are a kind of modified hair, consisting on the inside of a complex network of air chambers and attached to the muscle by a ball-shaped follicle. These quills are not the same thing as a porcupine's spines. A hedgehog's quills aren't barbed, and they don't detach from the hedgehog when it attacks. Petting a hedgehog will feel kind of like petting a hairbrush— bristly as opposed to spiky. When the animal is relaxed, its quills will be laid flat against its back;

when it's anxious, they'll raise up, first around the face, then over the whole body. If a hedgehog feels especially threatened, he'll roll himself into a ball with the quills sticking straight out.

A hedgehog's quills aren't only for defense. If a hedgehog falls from a significant height, it will roll up into a ball and let the spines absorb the impact, allowing them to survive drops of up to 20 feet with no injuries (though you shouldn't test this with your hedgehog at home!). Quills can also be used to help the hedgehog kill its prey, especially snakes, which tend to wriggle even after they've been caught.

Hedgehogs throughout history

Since they frequently live in areas with people, hedgehogs have been a fixture in folk tales for most of human history. The ancient Romans made hedgehogs a part of their festival of *Februa*, using them to predict the weather. If a hedgehog emerged from its den on February 2nd and saw its shadow, that meant there would be six more weeks of winter. This myth was the basis of the Groundhog Day rituals familiar in North America—since no hedgehogs live on this continent, the early American settlers substituted the closest rodent they could find. In the Middle Ages, various parts of the hedgehog were used medicinally, prescribed for everything from hair loss to improving night vision. More practically, the dried skins of hedgehogs were used for carding wool, since the quills would dry like fine nails and proved useful for combing fibers. Some cultures historically considered hedgehogs to be food, and they're still considered a delicacy in some African countries.

Hedgehogs appear in folktales throughout Europe, Africa, and Asia. Some ancient Chinese civilizations regarded hedgehogs as sacred while Norwegians consider them a symbol of independent thinkers.

Northern European folk tales often depict hedgehogs as underdogs who never give up, persevering in the face of seemingly insurmountable trials. Though they're typically regarded positively, hedgehogs were killed as nuisances in 16th century England, where they were mistakenly believed to destroy crops, or thought to carry plagues and diseases in the same manner as rats. England's stance on the hedgehog softened by the 20th century and the animal is better known now for its appearance in popular stories, like Beatrix Potter's washer woman Mrs. Tiggly-winkle or the balls in the Red Queen's croquet game in *Alice in Wonderland*.

In the modern world, hedgehogs are a protected species in most countries. Capture and export of the animal for the pet trade are either forbidden or strictly limited, and all of the hedgehogs sold as pets in North America come from captive breeding programs.

Hedgehogs as pets

Though they may look like rodents, to get a better sense of their care and personality you can think of hedgehogs more like very small cats. They need a diet heavy in protein and light on grains—in fact, keepers will often feed them dry cat food as the bulk of their diet. Hedgehogs take readily to litter box training and are generally clean animals. Being nocturnal, hedgehogs will be most active between dusk and dawn—roughly 7pm to 7am—and are excellent pets for people with busy schedules, content to hang out on their own most of the time. Hedgehogs will get stressed out and cranky if you try to wake them up during the daytime, and if you want a pet you can play with 24/7, a hedgehog is not for you. People who work during the day often find the hedgehog's nocturnal habits work perfectly with their busy schedules. The pet will want to eat and play around the time you're getting home, and should still be awake when you're getting ready the next morning.

Unlike other small animals, hedgehogs produce no noticeable odors. Since their teeth don't grow throughout their life like a hamster's they won't chew on things so aggressively. They're independent and intelligent animals, and while they can form strong bonds with their keepers and be very affectionate, they do so on their own terms and appreciate a good amount of solitude to balance the interaction.

Of course, hedgehogs aren't exactly like cats. The main difference is their environment. The hedgehogs sold as pets come from a hot, arid climate, and they need an ambient temperature between 70° and 90°F to stay healthy. They're also very active, with a territory of up to 1000 feet in the wild, and require a relatively large enclosure along with regular play and exercise time outside their cage. One advantage they have over larger pets is that they don't shed as much fur (though they do occasionally shed quills), and they don't trigger most pet allergies. People who are allergic to hedgehogs are typically allergic to the animal's saliva, meaning this allergy will only be triggered by handling the animal, not by simply sharing their space. In general, they're a lower maintenance pet than a cat or a dog, but that doesn't mean you can just stick the cage in the corner and forget it's there. Hedgehogs that don't get daily attention from their humans have a tendency to turn mean and anti-social. They can be wary of loud noises or aggressive attention, and thrive under the care of a patient and gentle keeper. Hedgehogs don't require any initial shots or immunizations, and while it is possible to spay a female "hedgie" it's a stressful procedure that's generally not done unless there's a reproductive health issue.

Hedgehogs weren't bred and sold in large numbers until the last quarter of the 20th century. Stores and veterinarians classify them as exotic pets and are not as familiar with their care and physiology as with those of more common animals. You may have some difficulty finding a vet nearby who's willing to treat your pet hedgehog. Since they are a more esoteric pet, you'll need to do more research into products before going to the pet store. There aren't many products labeled for hedgehog use, and the things that are aren't necessarily the best; your hedgehog's supplies will be a mix of those designed for rabbits, chinchillas, cats, and even reptiles. The trick is figuring out which things to get in each section. The recent introduction of the hedgehog captive breeding program also means they're closer to wild animals than most of the pets you can find at the store. The first wild-caught hedgehogs to be sold as pets could only be handled with gloves because they constantly had their quills raised and would hiss and bite at anyone who came near. Modern pet hedgehogs are bred to be more sociable, but there are still some captive-bred individuals that don't care to be handled much by humans. Because of this, it's very important to meet the individual hedgehog you plan to adopt before making your decision.

Legality

While hedgehog ownership is legal in the US and Canada on a federal level, there are some states, provinces, and cities that have banned ownership. As of the writing of this book, it is illegal to own a hedgehog in California, Hawaii, Pennsylvania, and parts of British Columbia, Ontario, and Virginia. Georgia allows licensed hedgehog breeders but not private pet ownership. Arizona doesn't explicitly outlaw hedgehogs, but the housing requirements to obtain a permit are difficult for even most zoos to meet, and for practical purposes you can consider them illegal. Other states require you to obtain a permit before purchasing an animal, including Maine, Montana, Nebraska, New Jersey, and Wyoming. If you're caught with an illegal pet you at least get a fine and may face jail time, and the animal will be taken away—sometimes to be moved out of state, more often to be euthanized. Even if you're not caught, no veterinarian in your state will be willing to see your animal if it's illegal, meaning a long journey if problems should arise.

Since these laws can change, you should check your area's policy regarding hedgehog ownership before buying an animal. Don't assume hedgehogs are legal just because you find them at the pet store. National pet store chains can sometimes inadvertently send animals to stores that shouldn't be selling them.

Life expectancy

Hedgehogs in the wild have a life expectancy of only 18-24 months, but hedgehogs in captivity live an average of 4-6 years and have been known to reach the age of 10 if cared for well. A lot of people see this as a positive over other small pets, but it does mean you have to plan a bit further into your future than with a rodent like a hamster. Make sure you'll still want the pet—and be able to care for it effectively—for at least six years.

Cost

The hedgehog itself will likely be the most expensive part of your initial investment. A single baby hedgehog will cost anywhere from $125-$350, depending on the color and gender. Females tend to cost more than males of the same color, since females are more in demand among breeders and are less likely to be born in the first place. The cage, toys, and other set-up supplies are going to vary widely in cost depending on the style and complexity of your setup, but you should plan on spending somewhere between $100 and $200. You should also plan on spending around $50 on an initial vet visit soon after bringing your pet home. Adding it all up, the up-front investment will be in the neighborhood of $300.

Ongoing costs of hedgehog care are relatively minimal. Depending on which brand you buy, you'll probably spend around $15-$25 per month on dry kibble. Aside from that, there are a lot of "ifs" involved in ongoing expenses. If you use recycled paper or wood shavings for bedding, you'll need to replace them at least once a month. These beddings typically cost between $10 and $25 per bag, though you'll likely only need 3-4 bags per year (depending on the messiness level of your hedgie). If you use a litter box, you'll need to buy litter ($10-$25 per bag), though you won't need to use much. The only major expense associated with hedgehog ownership is the potential for high vet bills as the pet ages. Older hedgehogs are prone to both kidney disease and cancer, the treatment for which can cost over a thousand dollars.

European vs. African hedgehogs

The majority of hedgehogs bred in North America are African pygmy hedgehogs, which are themselves a hybrid of two wild African species—the 4-toed or white-bellied hedgehog (*Atelerix albiventris*) and the Algerian hedgehog (*Atelerix algirus*). As the name pygmy would suggest, these animals are on the small side, typically weighing 300-700 grams and measuring 6-9 inches in length. Though many color variations are possible, the traditional coloration is a white-furred belly with black and white banded quills.

The hedgehogs featured in folk tales are typically Western or European hedgehogs (*Erinaceus europaeus*) or Eastern European hedgehogs (*Erinaceus concolor*). These animals have brown fur and quills and are generally larger, weighing up to 1000 grams and measuring 12-15 inches. These animals are rarely seen in the North American pet trade but may be familiar to European homeowners, who often aim to attract wild hedgehogs to their gardens to eat slugs, snails, and other pests. Both species of European hedgehog are threatened and protected in most of their range. Interacting with them in the wild is fine, but it may be illegal to capture and keep the animal, and you should allow it to stay in its natural habitat. Even the states where hedgehog ownership is legal may not also apply that to European species—since they're adapted to a temperate climate, they're more likely to become invasive if released in large enough numbers (as their introduction to New Zealand can attest to).

There's a bigger difference between these species than the color of their quills. European hedgehogs are accustomed to cold winters, which they pass by hibernating. This also means they're adapted to eating a fattier diet, especially in the fall when they're stocking up for their long sleep. African hedgehogs live in a climate where it's warm all year. They're active in all seasons and require a primarily protein-based diet that's very low in fat. Though they retain the instinct to hibernate when the temperature drops too much, they're not physiologically adapted for the process. Their speedy metabolisms don't slow enough, even in a state of torpor, and hibernation is often fatal for African hedgehogs.

Since they are by far the most common species found in the pet trade, the advice in this book is aimed at African pygmy hedgehogs. Don't assume your hedgehog is European just because it's brown. Some African hedgehogs are selectively bred for brown, tan, or orange colorations. If you're not sure of the origin of your new pet, you should ask the breeder to explain the animal's lineage. Most breed selectively and track the ancestry of their animals back at least five generations.

Behavior and personality

Some hedgehogs are explorers, boldly forging into new territory and constantly trying to escape from their cage. Others are cuddlers, perfectly content to pass an evening resting in their human's lap. Still more are loners who may be eager to solve mazes and puzzles but will hiss at the touch of an unwanted human hand. Even within the same litter, the personalities of individual hedgehogs vary widely, and it's very important to spend some time with the animal before you decide to adopt it.

That being said, the average hedgehog tolerates handling but rarely looks for attention. Hedgehogs are solitary in the wild, only coming together to mate. They won't get lonely without other hedgehogs around—in fact, they do best when housed singly. Male hedgehogs should never be kept in the same enclosure with another animal, male or female. Two or more females can usually cohabitate peacefully but should be carefully monitored and separated if they begin to fight.

Hedgehogs communicate through both body language and vocalizations. A content hedgehog will have smooth, flat quills and make a whistling or purring noise, or a pig-like snuffling sound that's especially common when they're foraging for food. An annoyed or nervous hedgehog will make puffing or snorting noises and erect the quills on its forehead over its eyes. Consider this a yellow light—move slowly, gently, and cautiously if you continue interacting. If all of a hedgehog's quills are erect, and it's hissing or clicking, the hedgehog is either scared or angry and you should leave it alone. He may also jump or "pop" when he's feeling especially grumpy. A well-treated hedgehog should rarely curl up into a tight ball. This is a defensive posture and a sign the hedgehog feels threatened. If the hedgie's curled into a loose ball and you can still see his face, he's just resting and all is well. When they're afraid, angry, or in pain, hedgehogs are capable of producing extremely loud screaming sounds. This is a cry for help and you should immediately find the source of the hedgehog's alarm.

One odd hedgehog behavior that deserves special attention is the practice of self-anointing. Hedgehogs are extremely odor-sensitive and when they encounter a particularly pungent or pleasant smell they'll start foaming at the mouth and then spread saliva over their quills. No one's completely sure why hedgehogs do this. Some speculate it's a form of camouflage to make the animal smell like its environment. Others think it's an attempt to increase the effectiveness of their quills by coating them with toxins. Whatever the reason, it's a perfectly normal hedgehog behavior and shouldn't be a cause for alarm. The unsubstantiated claim that hedgehogs frequently have rabies is likely due to a misunderstanding of this behavior, since foaming from the mouth is a common symptom of that disease.

Hedgehogs and other pets

You should supervise interactions between hedgehogs and larger pets, at least for the first few weeks the animal's in your home. A dog's curious pawing can injure a hedgehog just as much as an outright predatory attack from a cat. Luckily for the hedgehog, his quills will usually deter both kinds of attention. Though you want to make sure your enclosure is secure, most of the time cats and hedgehogs come to a kind of truce—after the first time your cat gets a paw full of quills, they'll usually leave the hedgehog alone (though they may sit and watch the hedgehog for hours, which could stress the little guy out). Interactions with dogs tend to be trickier. A large dog, especially, may try to pick the hedgehog up in its mouth, or bat it around like a ball. These actions are rarely aggressive or predatory in nature, but they can be equally harmful. Keep your dog's personality in mind before allowing the hedgehog to run around with it in an open space. Calm dogs often ignore or gently sniff at hedgehogs. More manic breeds may never learn how to interact with hedgehogs safely.

Surprisingly, ferrets tend to be the most dangerous animal common in a home. The ferret's strong natural odors will intrigue the hedgehog, while its sharp teeth and claws could cause the hedgie serious injury even if they're only trying to play. Shared playtime between the hedgehog and other small animals—like rabbits, guinea pigs, and rats—should be fine, though you should never house multiple species of small animal in the same enclosure.

Hedgehogs and children

Hedgehogs are not a good pet for small children. Their hands are too small to hold the hedgehog effectively—they'll likely grab on to quills, which could sting and make the child drop the animal. Children also have a tendency to hold on too tight, and a hedgehog is likely to bite if squeezed. The regular schedule of care a hedgehog requires can also be difficult for a younger child to keep up with, and an adult in the house should always supervise the care of a hedgehog owned by a child to make sure it's getting everything it needs. Generally speaking, hedgehogs are best for older teens or adults.

Since they sleep during the day, hedgehogs are also bad as classroom pets. Even a friendly hedgehog will be grumpy if you wake it up in the middle of the day. They also prefer a quieter, more peaceful environment—the grasping hands and screaming voices of a classroom of children won't give it an especially calm home space.

Vacations and travel

Any kind of relocation is very stressful on an animal. If you're going on vacation, it's best to leave the hedgehog in its cage at home and hire a pet sitter rather than taking it to a kennel or bringing it with you. Air travel can be especially brutal. Even if the airline lets you keep the animal in the cabin, the ambient air temperature on a plane is often too low for a hedgehog to stay comfortable. Especially long flights could send a hedgehog into potentially fatal hibernation.

If you have to travel with your hedgehog—if you're moving, for example, or need to take him to the vet—you can buy either a soft- or hard-sided pet carrier. Cat carriers work well for this. Include some scraps of a comfortable material, like fleece or flannel, so the hedgehog can curl up in them and feel safe. If it's cold out, you want to include some kind of heat source. A hot water bottle or chemical hand warmers wrapped in a towel will work, or a heating pad set on low under one corner of the carrier.

Other concerns

Like most animals, hedgehogs can carry illnesses and bacteria that can be transmitted to humans. The most noteworthy of these is salmonella. You should wash your hands after handling your hedgehog or cleaning its cage, and shouldn't allow it to walk on or inhabit areas where food is prepared. Anyone with a weakened immune system should not clean the cage.

Hedgehogs occasionally lose quills throughout their life, the same way people occasionally lose hairs. The difference is a human hair won't hurt if you find it with your bare feet. Even if you're conscientious when interacting with your hedgehog you'll find shed quills in the strangest of places, from the sheets of your bed to the cushion of the couch.

Buying a Hedgehog

Pet stores

A pet store may be your most convenient option for buying a hedgehog. You're more likely to find healthy hedgehogs and knowledgeable staff at a pet store specifically aimed at exotic pets than a large, more general shop. It's unfortunately rare to find a large pet store that treats its hedgehogs well. Too often, they're kept in overcrowded enclosures by staff with limited knowledge of their dietary and environmental needs. Baby hedgehogs in pet stores are often weaned too early—sometimes as young as 3 weeks, about half the time they're supposed to stay with their mother. The long-term impact of early weaning on the animal's health often can't be undone. If you buy your animal from a pet store, make sure to check out the cage where it's being housed. If the cage is dirty, overcrowded, or lacks sufficient food, water, and hiding places, you should not buy your hedgehog there. The animal will likely have health issues that could mean costly vet bills down the line, and it's likely to be improperly socialized (the grasping hands of so many strangers may make the animal permanently wary of handling). You might feel compelled to rescue the animal from deplorable conditions, but remember the business aspect of the pet trade. If you buy this animal, you're giving this shop your money, and supporting their continued mistreatment of small animals.

If you do buy an animal from a pet store, it's advisable to buy a male instead of a female. Though it's not healthy for female hedgehogs to breed before 5 months of age, they're sexually mature as early as 8 weeks. A lot of pet stores will let males and females cohabitate when they're young assuming no breeding can take place. Add the fact that it's extremely difficult to tell when a female hedgehog's pregnant, and you could end up bringing home the hedgie equivalent of a teenage mother. Aside from the health complications from this (and the fact that you now have 4-10 pets when you planned on having one) this often means hedgehogs are breeding with their siblings and can result in inbred offspring. Inbreeding leads to both psychological and physiological issues. If the pet store staff has trouble differentiating between male and female animals, you shouldn't buy a hedgehog there.

Breeders

A reputable breeder is the best place to buy your hedgehog. There are both good and bad breeders. The size of the operation is not the best indication of the quality—there are great large operations, and sub-par smaller ones. Like with pet stores, look at the enclosure where your hedgehog's being kept and make sure it's clean and not overcrowded. Be wary of any breeder who won't let you see the cages unless they give a good reason for the omission (e.g. there's a very pregnant female who shouldn't be disturbed, or a new litter of hoglets). Breeders are also the best place to look for specific color variants. The breeder should be able to provide at least five generations of lineage for your animal. This shows you two very important things: That the animal is not inbred, and that it's been selectively bred for a good personality. Generally speaking, hedgehogs bought from breeders are more accustomed to humans and friendlier overall.

A good breeder will be able to do more than simply sell you a pet. They'll be able to answer any questions you have about the animal's care and show you how to properly handle the hedgehog. You should also ask the breeder for recommendations on finding veterinary care. If they're willing to give you the name of their vet, this could be an ideal option—that vet may already have a relationship with your animal. If the breeder is unable to tell you where the closest vet is, that's a pretty big warning sign, because it means they're not taking the animals in for regular check-ups (if they simply can't give you that vet's information because he's full or only works with breeders, that's unfortunate but acceptable).

Rescue shelters

A rescued hedgehog is not the best pet for a first-time owner. These animals come with a history, and it's rarely a happy one. Improper nutrition and housing may have given it chronic health issues, which could translate to costly vet visits. Past neglect or bad experiences with handling could also make it standoffish or especially timid around people. A rescued hedgehog can take a long time to start trusting people again, and may never be as friendly as one bought young from a breeder.

The advantage of rescuing a hedgehog, of course, is that you're providing a home for an otherwise abandoned animal. If you feel up to the challenge, the International Hedgehog Association has a state-by-state listing of rescue organizations on their website (http://www.hedgehogclub.com/rescue/). Make sure you are prepared for the extra time and financial investment before adopting—you're not doing yourself or the animal any favors if you have to abandon it again because its care is more work than you expected.

Picking the right animal

Health and personality should be your two main factors in determining which hedgehog to buy. Though hedgehogs are good at hiding illnesses, there are several signs you should look out for when you're going to buy your new pet. Make sure the animal is moving easily, without a limp or any dragged limbs. The eyes should be bright and clear with no crusting or discharge; the ears should be smooth and rounded with no visible ear wax. Any sneezing, wheezing, or discharge from the nose is a sign of an infection. Check the skin between the quills for dry patches or sores and make sure the fur on the face and underbelly is soft and not matted. Hedgehogs should have no natural odor; if it smells bad, that's a sign of a dirty cage or serious illness. Any poop you see in the cage should be firm and dark brown. If it's green or slimy, the hedgehog likely has an intestinal illness or parasite. Even if these health issues are temporary, you shouldn't buy an animal that's sick. Moving causes the animal stress, weakening its immune system and making an existing condition get even worse.

Once you've determined the animal is physically healthy, you should assess his personality. Most hedgehogs will be a bit shy when faced with a new human, but he should unroll on your arm and relax his quills soon after you pick him up. An outgoing animal may immediately start exploring; a calmer one may simply sit on your arm and sniff you out. Both can be great pets. Decide whether you'd rather have an explorer or a cuddler and pick your animal accordingly. If you can, it's best to handle more than one animal before you make your decision. If the hedgehog jumps, pops, clicks, or hisses at you, you should put him back. This individual may just be having a bad day, but those could also be behaviors that never go away. You should be especially wary if multiple animals you pick up at the pet shop or breeder respond this way to your touch.

Age of a new hedgehog

Hedgehogs ideally should be left with their mothers until they're at least 6 weeks old. Beyond that, the age of the animal when you buy it is a matter of personal preference. Some breeders advise buying hedgehogs immediately after weaning. If the individual you buy is less than 12 weeks old, you'll have to deal with at least one quilling (more on that in chapter 4). A younger hedgehog will be more adaptable and if you plan on shifting its schedule to be more diurnal a younger hedgehog will respond better. Younger hedgehogs will also bond with new humans more readily. The advantage of buying a fully grown hedgehog (6 months or older) is that its personality will be fully developed and you'll be better able to assess what kind of pet it will be in the long term. If you're determined to buy a hedgehog with a specific personality, you should buy it as an adult.

Male vs. female

You can tell a hedgehog's gender easily by looking at its belly. Females will have 4-5 sets of little nipples running down their underside. Males will look like they have a "belly button" on their lower abdomen. This is the prepuce (penis housing) and will be separated from the anal opening.

Both male and female hedgehogs make good pets. There's no appreciable difference in personality between the two, in terms of their interaction with humans—there are outgoing females and shy males. Male hedgehogs will not get along with others of their kind, so if you want multiple hogs to have shared play time you should buy females. Neither males nor females produce any kind of musk, though male hedgehog urine may have a stronger odor. Male hedgehogs are typically less expensive than females, if that's a factor for you. In terms of health issues, females are more prone to reproductive issues (especially uterine cancers). These health concerns increase with breeding. Male hedgehogs have more issues with urinary tract infections, so the health concerns between genders ultimately balance out.

Chapter 2: Cage and Supplies

Despite their roly-poly appearance, hedgehogs in the wild are accustomed to running long distances and should be provided ample opportunities for exercise and exploration in captivity. Hedgehogs provided with inadequate exercise tend to one of two behavioral extremes: Either they will become reclusive and anti-social or they will spend much of their time awake running their nose along the inside of their cage and gnawing at the wires, sometimes to the point of causing themselves injury. Obesity is also a major concern for a hedgehog whose cage is too small. These effects are cumulative; hedgehogs become sicker, more aggressive and less friendly the longer they're deprived of sufficient physical and intellectual stimulation.

Set up your new pet's cage before you bring him home—moving is stressful for any creature and you want to limit the amount of time he spends in transition. Having the cage ready before the hedgehog's arrival also lets you perfect its placement in the home and make any necessary adjustments. If you own other pets, this also gives you an opportunity to test the security of the enclosure (an especially valuable step with cats).

Though they have gained popularity in the last few decades, hedgehogs are still considered an exotic pet, and as such you're unlikely to find a "hedgehog" section in your local pet store. To further complicate matters, certain brands have tried to jump on the bandwagon by marketing products to hedgehog owners without doing proper research into the animal's true dietary and environmental needs. Always check labels and use a critical eye when buying toys, bedding, or food for your hedgehog, and don't rely on the information given to you by pet store staff who likely received little (if any) specialized training in the exotic species their store carries. This advice is mainly aimed at large, multi-species pet stores; smaller shops specializing in exotic animals are more likely to be knowledgeable, and to stock their shelves with high-quality products.

The Cage

Your hedgehog cage should offer a minimum of four square feet of floor space. This is for a single animal; if you're planning on keeping more than one hedgehog in an enclosure, it will need to be larger to give both animals space to get away from you and each other (females only—remember that male hedgehogs should always be kept in solitary enclosures). Hedgehogs are accomplished climbers, and if floor space is an issue you could consider purchasing or making a multi-level home with ramps for navigation. Glass, hard plastic, and mesh are all great materials for your hedgehog's enclosure. Your main concern should be finding a cage that provides ample ventilation, prevents the hedgehog from escaping (or other animals from entering), and has a solid, level floor for the animal to walk on.

Guinea Pig Cages

Cages made for guinea pigs are often the perfect size for a hedgehog and are some of the few cages that can be used "out of the box" without modifications. Most models feature coated wire sides and top with a base of plastic, metal, or nylon. Make sure the floor is of a firm, solid material. If the wire bars of the cage start low enough for your hedgehog to climb them you may need to line the interior cage walls with thin pieces of a smooth, solid material.

Guinea pig cages are relatively inexpensive—simple models often cost less than $50. Coated wire cages in general have a similar pros and cons. They provide excellent ventilation and are lighter-weight than glass, but they can be difficult to clean thoroughly, especially around the edges and hinges, and the open sides mean you have to be very careful of temperature changes or drafts in the hedgehog's room.

Modified rabbit cages

The biggest difference between a rabbit cage and a guinea pig cage is that it's made for a larger animal and you have to be more careful of the width of the gaps between the bars. Look for bars that are spaced no more than ½-inch apart. A rabbit's larger feet also have an easier time on metal mesh floors that a hedgehog's paws can slip through. If you do buy a cage with a wire mesh floor, you'll need to cover it with a firm, solid material.

While it's not advisable to house your hedgehog outside full-time, rabbit hutches can make great outdoor playpens. Just keep careful watch around the edges of open-bottomed models that sit directly on the grass—hedgehogs love to burrow, and may just dig their way out into the open while you're not looking.

Modified ferret cages

Ferret cages come in a wide range of designs, from simple single-level cages with shelves and hammocks to elaborate 4-story modular towers. Ferret cages can be great for active hedgehogs but tend to need a few safety upgrades. Make sure that all ramps are at least as wide as your hedgehog's body—a bit of clearance on either side is always better—and that there are no steep drops from ledges or off of the edges of platforms (if there are, you can construct impromptu walls with nylon or sheets of plastic). Ferret habitats are the most expensive housing option on this list, running upwards of $250 for a multi-level cage.

Glass Aquaria

Though you typically find them in the fish or reptile section, glass aquaria also make excellent hedgehog enclosures. Look for an aquarium that's a 30-gallon long or larger capacity. If there are young children or other pets living in the home, a mesh screen top for the cage is a must. If there aren't, a screen top is optional but recommended—your hedgehog won't be able to climb the glass sides to escape but may learn to scale their wheel or hide box.

Glass has the advantage of holding heat better than wire enclosures and may be the best material for colder climates. Aquariums are easy to clean and relatively inexpensive. On the downside, they don't allow for as much ventilation. Glass is also heavy, making the enclosure difficult to move. There might also be a logistical issue fitting cage furnishings into an aquarium. Water bottles may be difficult to mount and exercise wheels are often too tall for a standard glass aquarium, though "flying saucer"-style wheels will fit comfortably.

Making your own cage

Even the best commercial enclosures will often need some kind of tweak before they're suitable for your hedgehog—so why not cut out the middle man and just make the cage yourself? Lots of exotic pet hobbyists do this since it allows you to construct a cage that's perfectly suited for your home and pet.

The best material options for doing it yourself cages are the same as for commercial models: Glass, hard plastic, and metal bars or mesh. Avoid wood and soft plastics because they can be more difficult to clean and disinfect. If you're going with metal, avoid anything containing zinc or lead as these minerals can cause toxicity in small animals. Any paints used in the cage decoration should also be non-toxic and lead-free, even if it's just on the outside.

The design possibilities when you're making your own cage are nearly endless and can be tailored to suit both your needs and those of your pet. You can create very cool modular enclosures using plastic storage containers linked together by PVC pipe. Simply buy a couple large-sized Steralite (or other clear plastic) storage containers and a length of PVC pipe with a 4" diameter. Cut the middle out of the container's lid and cover it with wire mesh to give the hedgehog more ventilation. Cut a hole in the side of each container, low enough for your hedgehog to get up inside, then attach the PVC pipe to each enclosure with aquarium sealant or another non-toxic glue. These kinds of cages can be especially good if you're housing multiple females together—when one of them needs alone time, you can simply close off the PVC pipe and separate the animals with little stress.

If you're looking for design inspiration, the forums over at Hedgehog Central have some great DIY project ideas (http://wiki.hedgehogcentral.com/tiki-index.php?page=DIY#Cages).

Heat and humidity

African hedgehogs are accustomed to living in a hot climate, and you want to replicate this to some extent to keep your hedgehog healthy. Aim to keep your cage's interior temperature in the 75°-80°F range. Older hedgehogs (starting around age five) will need a hotter environment (80°-84°F). A good rule of thumb is that if you're comfortable in a t-shirt, it's warm enough for a hedgehog. In the extremes, hedgehogs should get no colder than 70°F and no warmer than 90°F.

A thermometer is the best way to get an accurate reading of the temperature in your hedgehog's cage. Avoid the stick-on thermometers you can find at pet stores; these are notoriously inaccurate and will ultimately do more harm than good by potentially giving you a false sense of security (or alarm, depending on what it's reading). Digital thermometers with an external probe are the best for small animal owners. You may find these in the reptile or fish section of larger pet stores; if not, you should be able to find one at a home improvement store for less than ten dollars.

Heat and Lighting

Keeping your hedgehog's day/night cycle consistent is one of the best ways to keep him healthy in the long-term, and the easiest way to do this is with a light fixture hooked up to a timer. Hedgehogs do best with a year-round photoperiod of 12-16 hours of daylight and 8-12 hours of darkness. Even if you live in a warm environment and your hedgehog doesn't require an external heat source, you still need to provide them with a consistent photoperiod. Aberrations in their daily light schedule can cause insomnia and illness, and may trigger attempts at hibernation.

A hedgehog's lighting needs are much easier to accommodate than those of cold-blooded animals like lizards and turtles. There is no evidence that hedgehogs require UV exposure, meaning your pet will not require fluorescent or mercury vapor lighting. While your lighting can provide extra heat for hedgehogs in cold climates, they do not require a basking area the way reptiles do. You should not rest the fixture directly on the cage—metal cages, especially, conduct heat exceptionally well and could easily cause burns. Mount the bulb near the cage but not touching it and carefully monitor the temperature. You can use a standard incandescent bulb to give your hedgehog the daylight it needs. Even if he spends the entire day in his burrow sleeping, his body and brain will recognize the light as "day" and keep his metabolism accordingly regulated.

Night bulbs

Owning a nocturnal pet can be frustrating. You want to give him the day/night cycle he needs but still be able to enjoy his company. Night viewing bulbs can often help with this. These are infrared or ultraviolet bulbs that produce a red, purple, or blue light, and you can find them in the reptile section of most pet stores. While some hedgehogs are very particular and will only come out and play in complete darkness, most respond well to these night-viewing bulbs. Keep a close eye on the hedgehog after you introduce a night bulb to his habitat, paying special attention to any changes in behavior. If he gets agitated, reclusive, or lethargic, you should stop using the night bulb—however convenient it may be for observing your pet, the animal's health always comes first.

Other heating methods

If you need to provide extra heat, a standard heating pad on the lowest setting placed underneath the cage should be sufficient to raise the temperature. Put it under only one side of the cage so your animal can get away from the heat if it wants to. If your cage base is plastic and you're concerned about it melting, a space heater in the hedgehog's room can also work nicely. If you use a space heater, make sure it's not pointed directly at the hedgehog's enclosure—though the air coming out of a space heater is warm, it's still moving air and can cause a draft, creating the opposite effect that you're looking for.

Don't heat tape, heat rocks, or undertank heaters marketed for reptile use, for the same reason that you don't want to set up a basking light. These products are designed to raise the temperature to comfortable levels for cold-blooded critters, typically somewhere in the range of 90°-110°F—much too warm for a

hedgehog.

Bedding

Bedding for a hedgehog serves multiple purposes.
It gives the animal traction and protects their feet
from the hard surface of the cage floor. It also absorbs
the animal's waste and any spilled food and water.
Finally, it serves as nesting material, and you'll find
your hedgehog will like to mound it up inside his hide
box burrow down inside of it (if you use a bedding
that allows them to do so). There's a wide variety of
bedding options on the market and a few equally
attractive do it yourself options that are worth
considering.

First, we should talk about which things make
inadequate beddings. Products made of corn cob can
cause problems with hedgehogs, especially males,

who have been known to get pieces of the bedding stuck in their prepuce. These beddings also tend to rot and mildew when wet, causing unpleasant odors and promoting bacterial growth inside the cage. You should also avoid any bedding made of cedar or pine shavings. Cedar contains Plicatic Acid, an aromatic and potentially toxic substance that has been known to trigger allergies in humans and small animals alike and could damage the hedgehog's skin, respiratory system, and liver. Other pines get their great scents from similar abietic acids. Just like with people, some hedgehogs are going to be more sensitive to these compounds than others. Some breeders use cedar shaving beddings with no issue, but there's no telling how your individual hedgehog will react. There're so many other great options available that it's just not worth the risk. If you're going the cage liner route, avoid thin, plush fabrics like vellux. This material is soft but not very durable and a hedgehog's natural tendency to burrow will destroy the liner quickly.

Cage Liners

Fleece or flannel cage liners are excellent bedding options. You can buy them pre-made from breeders and hobbyists online. Measure the interior of your cage and buy one that's flush against the edges; commercial cages come in a standard range of sizes and you should be able to find a liner that fits with little searching. Look for one that's got two layers of fleece with some kind of padding in the center, and make sure there are no frayed edges or stray threads that the hedgehog's feet could get caught in. If you go with a cage liner you should put a paper towel or piece of newspaper underneath it. As opposed to other beddings that are valued for their absorbency, fleece makes an excellent liner because it's hydrophobic—it can't hold more than 1% of its mass in water, meaning urine flows right through it and won't pool or cause wet spots in the liner.

If your hedgehog is not litter box trained, you'll need to change the liner every day; if he is, you'll still have to change it 2-3 times per week. Even a litter box trained hedgehog will release waste while he's running on his wheel, so pay special attention to this area of the liner when deciding whether it's time to change it.

If you use cage liners, you need to have a minimum of two (one to put in the cage while the other is being cleaned). If the pet's not litter trained and you don't want to have to wash a cage liner every day, you could get a set of 8 liners—a fresh one for each day, plus one to keep in the cage while you wash the rest. This makes cage liners a larger initial investment, but since they're washable and reusable they'll be cheaper in the long term. Cage liners are comfortable and sanitary, but they don't allow the hedgehog to burrow. If you notice your pet trying to burrow underneath the liner, you could put a few scraps of fleece in for him to dig under, or some shredded newspaper or recycled paper that can serve as nesting materials in the hide box.

Recycled Paper

Sold in the small animal section of most pet stores, recycled paper bedding is a great option for a hedgehog environment. It's soft, absorbent, and promotes a hedgehog's natural burrowing activity. The light color of most of these beddings makes it easy to see changes in your pet's urine or stool, allowing early detection of developing health issues. Fill the bottom of the cage to a depth of at least three inches. You can spot-clean recycled paper bedding reasonably well and should do so daily, replacing all the bedding on a monthly basis.

The main disadvantage of recycled paper beddings is the cost ($20-$30 for a 25-liter bag). If you've got more time than money, you could make your own recycled paper bedding at home out of junk mail and scrap paper. Remove any glossy pages or non-paper components (plastic or glue from envelopes, staples from magazines, etc) then tear the paper sheets in half and soak in a large container of lukewarm water. Use your fingers to swirl the paper scraps around, tearing them into smaller chunks as you go until the water is too gray to see your hands. Drain your paper and repeat the process four or five times then rinse the paper until squeezing a chunk of pulp makes clear water run out. Form the pulp into baseball-sized chunks, break them into small scraps, and allow them to dry. It's a time-consuming process but it's eco-friendly and cost-effective, and can be a fun project to do with small children if they want to be a part of the hedgehog's care.

Wood shavings

Shavings of woods other than cedar or pine can be a good bedding choice for hedgehogs. Aspen is the most popular choice and what you'll likely find in your local pet shop. Like recycled paper, wood shaving offers the advantage of being relatively soft and encouraging natural burrowing behavior. Also like recycled paper, you should fill the bottom of the tank to a depth of at least three inches, spot cleaning daily and fully replacing at least once a month.

While many breeders and keepers use aspen shavings as bedding, it does have some disadvantages. Though aspen hasn't been implicated in respiratory or liver issues like cedar has, certain individuals—human and hedgie alike—are more prone to skin allergies than others and may have a reaction from any wood-based bedding. If your hedgehog is scratching or biting itself more frequently than normal, consider changing his bedding material. Some people also avoid wood shavings because of the sharp edges of the wood, which do open up the potential for a hedgehog to poke himself in the eye or give himself splinters when he's navigating his cage. Most hedgehogs won't have this problem—they frequently contend with organic debris in the wild—but if your pet falls off his wheel a lot or seems especially injury-prone, you may want to go with a softer, smoother bedding.

Pellet beddings

While not as soft as recycled paper, pellet-form commercial beddings are arguably the most absorbent item on this list and are used very effectively by many keepers and breeders. This may be your best bedding option if you have one of the rare hedgehogs who refuses to use a litter box. Though pellets are heavier than recycled paper, your hedgehog should still be able to burrow comfortably; like the above options you should fill the bottom of the cage to a depth of three inches to allow this. Unlike recycled paper or wood, pelleted beddings aren't going to provide good nesting material. On the plus side, most pelleted beddings are compostable and flushable in the quantities you'll be removing in your daily spot-cleaning, making disposal easier, and they're generally a very eco-friendly option.

Cage Placement

You want to pick a room for your hedgehog where he can get daily attention and observation from his humans without being disturbed during his normal sleeping hours by excessive noise or vibrations. For most people this will be an easy requirement to satisfy, since the hedgehog's normal sleeping hours will coincide with the time you're away at work or school. A home office, den, or family room could all be ideal places for your new pet.

Children may want to keep the hedgehog in their bedroom, but this is a generally a bad idea. Depending on the child's age, you run the risk of the hedgehog being forgotten. While most bedrooms are nice and quiet during the day, the more time your hedgehog spends smelling and hearing people around him, the more comfortable he'll be interacting with them. Also remember that hedgehogs are by nature nocturnal, and will likely be up all night searching for food and running around his cage. There is no such thing as a silent exercise wheel—a fact that you'll become painfully aware of every night if you plan on sleeping just a few feet from a hedgehog's cage.

Once you've narrowed down the room where your hedgehog will live, you should be equally careful about where you position it. Keep the cage away from any windows, which can cause problems on both ends of the temperature spectrum—the glass amplifies sunlight and may heat the cage too much, while drafts can make the cage too cool. Also avoid putting the cage in front of heating vents or air conditioners— anywhere there might be a significant amount of air movement. If you're not sure whether an area is drafty or not, light a candle and hold it in the space where your cage is going to be. If the flame flickers, the area is drafty and unsuitable for your hedgehog cage; if the flame is relatively still, the area will work.

Exercise Wheels

Hedgehogs are accustomed to running long distances in their natural habitat, and a high-quality exercise wheel is necessary for a captive hog to thrive. Traditional hamster wheels (a wire mesh wheel open on both sides mounted on an axle connected to triangular supports) are not suitable for hedgehogs; in fact, these models exemplify exactly what you don't want. The supports are the first problem. Many hedgehogs like to step off of their wheels mid-run, and the external frame could injure or trap them in the process, while their backs often bump into the central axle while they're running. The wire mesh wheel often catches hedgehog toes and quills, causing injury. These models can also be top-heavy and are prone to toppling when climbed on.

The ideal hedgehog wheel has a 12" diameter with a running tread that's 4-6" wide. The wheel should be of a solid material and can be made of either metal or plastic so long as it has enough tread. The entry side should be free of obstruction. To avoid potential falls, the wheel can be attached to the side of the cage or firmly mounted to a weighted or secured base. There are a few different designs that satisfy all these requirements, some of which are radical departures from what you might picture when you think of an exercise wheel.

Regardless of which design you pick, make sure that it can be easily cleaned and removed. Even for litter box trained pets the wheel often serves as a backup bathroom. Running stimulates a hedgehog's metabolism and causes his body to expel waste. Instinct tells the hedgehog he's leaving the waste behind as he runs and he won't show his usual concern for cleanliness. Wheels should be wiped down daily as part of your maintenance routine. Remove and disinfect the wheel at least once a month.

Bucket wheels

Made of solid, durable plastic, bucket wheels are often made and sold by breeders and hobbyists, and they're available in a range of styles and sizes online. You can fasten it to the side of the cage or mount it on a stand; it will be quiet and take up very little floor space. The only issues with bucket wheels are that you're unlikely to find them at your local pet store, and they can be costly ($20-$30 before shipping).

Flying saucer wheels

The flying saucer is an exercise wheel flattened and turned on its side. They feature a broad, textured disc mounted at an angle on an attached stand. They are safe, quiet, and easy to clean. Though they take up a lot of floor space inside the cage, they are great for enclosures with a low clearance. They're a little trickier to use; most hedgehogs don't take long to figure them out but older hedgehogs may have difficulty, and they might be hard to use for especially large animals. The main disadvantage keepers find in flying saucer style wheels is that they can fling the waste your pet drops while running around the cage if they build up enough speed, causing quite a mess.

Chinchilla wheels

Solid wheels designed for chinchillas—like the steel Quality Comfort models and the all-plastic Comfort Wheels—can be great options for longer and larger hedgehogs. Both models are a bit noisier, generally, than the styles listed above. The plastic Comfort Wheels may be more difficult to clean because of the grooves on the running surface and you should keep a close eye on your hedgehog's feet when he's using this kind of wheel (he may run them raw). The solid steel models have a smooth surface but you should check the outer edge frequently to make sure there're no sharp edges. The main issue with both styles of chinchilla wheels is that they can be top-heavy and have been known to topple. Affixing these wheels to the side of the cage is the best and safest option.

Other furnishings and necessities

Hide box

Since they sleep during daylight hours, hedgehogs are accustomed to hiding when it's time for them to sleep. In the wild, they'll rest under leaves, shrubs, or rocks—pretty much in any crevice they can find. This means they won't be especially picky about what you give them as a hiding area. Hedgehogs enter their burrows headfirst, so you need to make sure the area inside is big enough for the animal to comfortably turn around. The entrance should be wide enough for the hedgehog to enter but narrow enough to limit the light that comes in.

Hide boxes are one of the few hedgehog supplies you can find readily at any major pet store. Plastic "igloo"-style hiding areas are great—buy one sized for small rabbits or chinchillas; the hamster and gerbil sizes will be too small. Cork bark and hollowed-log hides designed for lizards can also work great for hedgehogs. All of these options cost $10-$20, depending on the shop and style.

There are also a lot of common household items that make excellent hedgehog hiding areas. A simple flipped over cardboard box with a hole cut in the side for entrance will work, though you won't be able to clean it and will have to replace it when the cardboard gets wet or messy. A clay or ceramic flower pot turned on its side can also work, or a piece of PVC pipe with an interior diameter of at least 4 inches—pretty much anything that's got a large enough interior and is made of non-toxic materials. Just like with the bedding, avoid anything made of cedar or pine, or metals containing zinc and lead.

You should provide your hedgehog with soft material inside the hide to let them sleep comfortably. If you're using recycled paper as your main bedding, this should suffice—the hedgehog will mound up the recycled paper into a nest inside their hide box. If you're using other bedding materials, a small pile of nesting material should be provided. Hay, straw, and grass work great for this, as does recycled paper or scraps of an approved cloth, like flannel, corduroy, or fleece. If you use disposable options (hay, recycled paper, etc) replace the nesting material once a month. Scraps of cloth can be cleaned and re-used so long as they're not fraying on the edges. The frequency with which you'll need to wash them largely depends on whether or not your hedgie is litter box trained, but these cloth items should be washed at the least once every month and perhaps as frequently as once a week.

Litter box

Hedgehogs are naturally neat creatures, and even without a litter box you'll probably find them using one area of their cage most often to go to the bathroom. Because of this, most hedgehogs adapt readily to litter box use with very little training. Work with your hedgehog's natural instincts in this regard. Note where he is choosing to go to the bathroom (this will probably be on the lowest level of the cage in one of the corners) and put the litter box in that area. The majority of the time, the hedgehog will start using it without missing a beat. If your hedgehog seems confused or shows resistance, try cleaning his cage and replacing the bedding, then putting a small amount of soiled bedding inside the litter box. The smell of it should draw your hedgie in. Alternatively, if there are multiple hedgehogs in your household, you could put a small amount of another hedgehog's soiled bedding in the litter box—male hedgehogs, especially, will be eager to cover up that scent with their own. Rarely, a hedgehog will reject litter box use. If you're dedicated and patient, you can sometimes get the point across by regularly moving waste from the rest of the cage into the box and gently showing the hedgehog where it is, but there are individuals who will turn their nose up at the litter pan regardless of attempts at training.

The litter pan can be metal, plastic, or ceramic/terra cotta. It should be about two inches deep and at least six inches on each side. Avoid traditional kitty litter inside the pan, especially the clumping or clay-based varieties. Most hedgies will roll in fresh litter and these materials have a tendency to stick to the quills and feet or inside reproductive openings. They also produce a lot of dust which can cause dry skin and irritate the lungs. Pellet-shaped litters (either made from plant matter or newsprint) are great options; recycled paper bedding can also work well. Pick something relatively light in color so you can see any abnormalities in the color and consistency of waste. If you're concerned about the odor, you can add a tablespoon of baking soda to the litter. Spot-clean the litter box daily with a litter scoop or designated slotted spoon, and clean the litter box— putting in completely fresh litter—once a week.

Food and water containers

You'll need three separate containers for feeding and watering your hedgehog: One for the dry food, one for treats and wet food, and one for the water. We'll deal with food dishes first because they're the simplest. What you're looking for is a low (no more than 3 inches tall) and bottom-heavy dish of about 3-6 inches in diameter. Ceramic and earthenware bowls work great for this. Metal and plastic are often less desirable—it's almost guaranteed that your hedgehog will climb on the food area and lighter-weight dishes will be flipped over and used as toys. If your set-up allows it, attaching dishes to the side of the cage will also help prevent this.

Regarding water, you have a couple of options. Some keepers use a standard plastic water bottle from the small animal section. These bottles have the advantage of being unlikely to spill, though you may get drips directly below the water bottle. Since it is less likely to spill you'll also get a more accurate sense of how much water your hedgehog is drinking, which can be helpful in tracking his health. Some hedgehogs don't like water bottles, though—water in bottles can sometimes pick up the taste or smell of the plastic and be unappetizing to the hog. You also have to be careful of where you position the water bottle and its holder. Hedgehogs love to climb and may figure out how to use the bottle as a ladder to escape. You could also use a ceramic dish like you use for the food. The open surface of the dish means it won't retain unusual odors or tastes that your hedgehog rejects. The main disadvantage is that it will almost certainly splash, and your pet will likely drag some bedding into the water, meaning the dish will need to be emptied and cleaned more often. Spilled water from a ceramic dish can raise the humidity inside the enclosure, as well, and if the cage isn't especially well ventilated this could become an issue.

The main concern when placing food and water dishes inside the cage is to keep them as far as possible from the litter box or designated bathroom area. The water and dry food dishes should be cleaned and re-filled daily, but otherwise should be left in the cage full-time. The wet food/treats dish should be removed and cleaned after each use.

Nail maintenance

You can limit the amount of trimming your hedgehog's nails require by providing him with a natural way to wear his nails down over the course of his day. You're looking for a hard material without any jagged edges—something like a low, flat stone, a piece of patio tile, or a clean-sided brick would work wonderfully. Place it well away from the wheel so your pet doesn't accidentally run into it during clumsy landings. A lot of keepers will put this piece of hard material under the food and water dishes. This allows it to serve multiple purposes—it elevates the dishes, making them less likely to become contaminated with bedding, and it provides another layer of protection between the food and the bedding to limit the mess from spills. Your hedgehog is also guaranteed to be walking in this area of his cage regularly so you'll know the nails will get lots of chances to file down.

Scale

Changes to your hedgehog's weight are one of the best early indicators of budding health issues, and it's a great idea to get a digital kitchen scale so you can keep track of this. Buy a digital scale that measures in increments of 1-2 grams so you can get a truly accurate reading—you can find these for around $30-$40 at a department store or kitchen supply store. Weigh your hedgehog once a month and keep a record of his weights so you can notice any trends or changes.

Play pen

Out of cage play time is necessary for a hedgehog's physical and intellectual stimulation. When you're going out to buy supplies for your new pet you should consider where they'll go when they're not in their cage. It should be noted that this is an optional expense. Many keepers have great success with letting their hedgehogs play in a closed-off room or stoppered bathtub. Those options, as well as safety considerations and toys, are discussed in more detail in the next chapter.

If you want to buy a playpen, you can get a metal or nylon model designed for rabbits, ferrets, or chinchillas. Just make sure the bars are spaced close enough together that the hedgehog can't slip between them; if the metal is a mesh, you may need to line it with some kind of plastic sheeting so the hedgehog can't climb up and out. These models are completely collapsible and adjustable and easy to set up or take down, making them great for homes with limited space. You can also find appealing options at a toy store. Hard plastic kiddie pools or sandboxes can work great. The advantage of these models is convenience—you can leave the toys in the space when you're not using them and don't have to set up and tear down the structure every time you want to play. The disadvantage is the amount of floor space they require.

Chapter 3: Handling and feeding

When you're living with an exotic animal, the first rule of thumb to keep in mind is that they're tame but they're not domestic. Most hedgehogs sold in today's pet trade are only a few generations removed from being wild and their survival instincts are much stronger than a cat's or dog's. The key to successful hedgehog ownership is to work with these instincts, allowing the hedgehog—whenever possible—to be the master of his own domain.

Hedgehogs are typically active from 7pm-7am. It may be possible to adjust this schedule with enough care and patience, but some individuals never fully adapt to new schedules and you have to be willing to let the pet stay active at night if that's what works best for him. Similarly, while some hedgehogs will be loving and affectionate, others will remain somewhat timid and reclusive no matter how often they're handled. There are introverts and extroverts in the hedgehog world just like there are in the human world, and you won't do yourself or your pet any favors by trying to force him to be something he's not.

Bringing your hedgehog home

Moving is a stressful process, for animals as well as people, and once you've got your new pet settled into his cage it's best to leave him alone for about 24 hours before trying to handle him. Give your new pet food and water and check on him a couple times to make sure he's eating and drinking; otherwise, leave him be.

If your hedgehog is not eating or drinking, you shouldn't panic right away. If you're using a water bottle, try switching to a dish. If you're using tap water, try a bottled water instead; the tap water in certain areas contains minerals that hedgehogs find unappetizing. If he won't eat, try calling the pet store or breeder where you bought the animal and asking what kind of food they use. It's possible there's just too much change happening at once and a touch of the familiar in his food dish could give your hedgie back his appetite. Count or weigh the kibble so you can accurately track whether he's eating or not; it's possible he won't eat while you're around until he's used to your presence. If the animal's generally active and he's passing solid waste, give him a few days—he might simply be adjusting. If he seems depressed or lethargic and his poop is green or slimy, you should call your vet.

Once his 24-hour adjustment period is over, the first thing you should do is get a baseline weight. Hedgehogs gain about an ounce a week for the first 12 weeks of life and continue growing until 6 months, at which point their weight should remain relatively consistent. The typical weight range for a healthy adult hedgehog is between 350 and 500 grams, but smaller animals can be healthy at as little as 250 grams, and larger individuals may weigh up to 1000. This is why it's best to keep a regular record of your hedgehog's weight and base health decisions on individual changes, not a set range.

Socializing your hedgehog

The amount of time it takes a hedgehog to get used to human action varies widely from one individual to another. In general, animals purchased from a breeder will be better socialized than those bought at a pet store—they're more likely to receive daily attention and individual handling, while pet store hedgehogs may have been subjected to rough or unwanted touching, and are often more wary of new humans at first.

A hedgehog's not as easy to pick up as some other pets. If he's feeling defensive or frightened, your hedgehog will either raise his quills or go into full-on ball mode. The more you handle your hedgehog, the more he'll get used to you and the less likely he'll be to prickle up at your approach. Normally you'll want to avoid handling the hedgehog when he's balled up, since this is a pretty clear sign he's in no mood to be touched. There are two exceptions to this rule: early in the ownership when the hedgehog's getting used to you and when the hedgehog escapes and you need to retrieve it. Keep a pair of heavy duty work or garden gloves on hand for this purpose.

In the first week, you should aim to handle your hedgehog for about half an hour every day. Pick up the animal by gently sliding your hands underneath it from the sides. You should feel fur under your fingertips instead of quills. Lift him out slowly and carefully; you can lean him on your forearm for support. For the first few interactions, you want to settle the hedgehog in your lap and let it get to know you at its own will. Outgoing hedgehogs will start exploring you within a couple of minutes. A shy hedgehog might stay tightly balled during your first interaction, or he may move only enough to bury his face in your elbow and hide. In either case, don't try to grab the hedgehog, and don't make too many fast movements. You can offer treats if he seems receptive to them. The goal is to give him positive associations with your scent and make him feel safe. If you want to speed the socialization along or if the animal's acting especially shy you can put an old t-shirt that's been recently worn in the cage as a blanket. Your scent will be on the shirt and the hedgehog will start to associate your smell with comfort.

Once he's actively exploring you and seems relatively comfortable with your presence you can try petting your hedgehog. This may happen on the first day, or it may not happen until the end of the first week; be patient if he seems reluctant to be touched. When you pet him, start with the rump, and only gradually work up toward the face. If the spines on his forehead start to go up or if he makes any kind of hissing noise, stop touching him and let him be. Eventually, most hedgehogs will climb up your limbs, sitting on your shoulder or even riding happily in a shirt pocket. Starting slow is the key to gaining this level of trust. After the hedgehog's adjusted, you can balance quiet together time with active play using toys or mazes, but you should continue to handle him every day when possible to maintain your relationship. An under-handled hedgehog will revert to moodiness and may lash out.

Introducing your pet to strangers

It can be tempting to want to show off your new hedgehog to everyone who comes to your house—it's exciting to get a new pet, and you want him to be a part of your family. You should resist this urge, though, and continue to introduce new people to your hedgehog slowly until you're sure how he'll react. Don't introduce your hedgehog to any strangers until he's completely comfortable with you. After you've reached this point, have a friend come over and start the same way you did—take the hedgehog out of its enclosure, settle him into the newcomer's lap, and instruct your friend not to attempt to touch or move him until he decides to begin exploring on his own.

Some animals can quickly reach the point of feeling comfortable with anyone and seem to love human attention; others bond very closely with a single handler and are wary of any other hands coming near. There's no way to tell which kind of hedgehog you have until you've seen him interacting with a variety of people. If it's especially important to you to find a gregarious hedgehog, you may want to get an adult individual from a breeder whose personality is fully known and developed.

Dealing with bites

Even well-adjusted hedgehogs occasionally bite, and it's something you should be prepared for. There are two kinds of bite: a playful nipping and a serious fear reaction. Nipping can happen during play or when feeding treats. As noted above, hedgehogs are very scent-sensitive and may lick and nibble on things it thinks smells or tastes good. If your hedgehog starts aggressively licking something it's priming to take a bite and you should move it—especially if that thing is your finger. Scents that hedgehogs find appealing include perfumes and colognes, so if you wear scented products on your wrists you may be at risk for nibbles. Salty things taste very good to hedgehogs; if you've recently eaten salty or savory snacks the taste of them might still be on your fingers. Tobacco smoke is another common cause of exploratory nibbles. Most hedgehogs will want to self-anoint with this aroma. The best way to prevent these kinds of exploratory bites is to wash your hands thoroughly before handling the animal. Even if he does nibble you, these kinds of nips rarely break the skin and are no more painful than a sharp pinch (though they should still be discouraged).

Fear or defensive bites are a more serious issue. These bites are more aggressive and typically do break the skin. To make matters worse, a hedgehog will often lock its jaws once it's bitten down. This is to prevent wriggling prey from escaping in the wild and can make bites very damaging and painful if they're not handled correctly. Don't try to tug the bitten item forward out of the hedgehog's mouth—you'll injure yourself, your pet, or both. To force the jaws to unlock, push the bitten item in toward the hedgehog's head. Stay as calm as you possibly can if your hedgehog bites you. Return it safely to its cage then wash and disinfect the wound.

If defensive biting becomes habitual, it's imperative that you find out the root of the problem. Make sure he's being handled gently by everyone. Hedgehogs differentiate between multiple owners by their scent and the sound of their voice, so look for patterns in the animal's aggressive behavior. If he's acting out because of improper handling, looking at who puts him on edge will help to identify the culprit. If he's biting everyone equally, it could be out of pain. Check his body for bruises or visible wounds, and make an appointment with the vet to make sure nothing's wrong. Also thoroughly inspect his cage to see if there's something inside of it causing discomfort.

If the hedgehog is being handled well and there's nothing wrong with him or his enclosure, there are a few methods you can try to curtail biting behaviors. A drop of rubbing alcohol on the hedgehog's nose when it bites will make it release. The animal will likely self-anoint with the odor but it won't harm him and he should stop biting with time. You could also blow gently in his face, or use a plant sprayer to gently mist his face when he appears to be preparing to bite. Don't turn to these methods until you're sure there's not a legitimate reason behind the habitual biting. You don't want to discourage your hedgehog from showing you when something's really wrong.

Food and nutrition

Hedgehogs are classified as insectivores, but in reality they're omnivores, opportunistic feeders who'll eat whatever happens along. Their diet in captivity should be high in protein and low in fat. While there are commercial hedgehog chow products available, many of these are simply re-packaged food for rodents, or the leftovers from making cat and dog food. In either case, these aren't appropriate diets for a hedgehog. Rodent diets rely too heavily on grains in their formula and won't give a hedgehog enough protein, while the leftovers of other animals food will be lacking in nutrients and too high in fat.

The bulk of your hedgehog's food should be comprised of hard kibble. The texture of the kibble will help the animal to keep its teeth clean and prevent dental issues. A healthy adult hedgehog will eat between ½ and 2 tablespoons of kibble a night depending on their age, activity level, and metabolism. You can adjust this amount to suit your individual hedgehog by keeping close watch of their weight and increasing or decreasing their food allowance accordingly. Make a mix for your hedgehog consisting of at least three different brands of kibble to make sure he's getting a good range of nutritional input. Supplement this chow with occasional fruits and vegetables, cooked meats, and insects like mealworms and crickets.

In the wild, hedgehogs do most of their foraging at dawn and dusk, and these are the best times to offer them food in captivity. Replace the dry food with fresh offerings at around 7pm and leave it in the cage all night. Treats should be given when you want the hedgehog to come out to play. You can split their daily feeding into 2-3 smaller sessions if you'd prefer; this may be helpful in adjusting their schedule to be more awake during the daytime. Make sure the food you offer is at room temperature or warmer when you give it to your hedgehog; this tends to make hedgehogs want to eat it more.

Hedgehogs are lactose intolerant and shouldn't be fed anything containing dairy. You should also avoid food that has artificial preservatives like BHA (butylated hydroxyanisole) and BHT (butylated hydroxytoluene) as these have been suspected of causing serious health problems, including certain cancers. Generally speaking, hedgehogs are resistant to most toxins, but there are a few foods that could be dangerous. Avoid avocados, grapes, and raisins— these foods have been linked to liver and renal failure. Nuts and seeds (frequent contributors to many small pet diets) are potential choking hazards and generally too fatty for a hedgehog; you should avoid feeding them. Anything a human would consider "junk food" is also bad. The high fat and sugar levels can contribute to obesity, and these foods often contain unhealthy preservatives.

There are a lot of good options for kibble at your local pet store that may or may not claim to be for hedgehogs. Always check the label on any food you buy and avoid anything with grain or corn as its primary ingredient, or anything that contains excessive amounts of preservatives, even if they're not the specific ones noted above.

For owners of multiple pet species: you should not allow your hedgehog to share a larger pet's dish, even if they eat exactly the same kind of food. This is partially to avoid cross-contamination of the food and prevent illness in all your animals, but it also prevents injury. Cats and dogs who are otherwise placid and accepting of the hedgehog might get protective of their food dishes, or could be so focused on eating that they step on or hit the hedgie without even meaning to (or noticing). It's also impossible to determine how much food each individual animal is eating if they're sharing dishes, meaning you won't be able to monitor your hedgehog's intake and could miss signs of an impending illness.

Dry cat or kitten kibble

Cat and kitten chows are the most reliable source of properly balanced nutrients. Look for a high-quality product that has meat as the primary ingredient. Meat or meat meal should also be the second ingredient listed. The kibble should ideally have 30% protein, though anything in the range of 24-35% is acceptable. Also look for a food that's less than 15% fat and low in iron. Young hedgehogs (under 10 weeks of age) should be fed kitten chow—it's soft, smaller, and easier for them to digest. After that, you can move them to a low-calorie formula for adult cats. The insects hedgehogs eat in the wild are very crunchy, and kibble delivers that crunch, making it appetizing for most hogs. Some will be picky about the shape or taste of their kibble once they've gotten used to a certain kind. If you're trying out a new pet food, ask the store if they have a sample bag you can try so you don't waste money on something your hedgehog will refuse to eat.

Dry dog food

Dog food meeting the same requirements (30% protein, 15% fat, low iron, and meat based) will fill your hedgehog's nutritional needs. Buy the type made for small dogs—larger pieces of kibble may be difficult for a hedgehog to get its mouth around and chew. If you already have a large dog that eats food nutritionally suitable for your hedgehog, you can break the larger kibble into smaller chunks in the food processor and offer it to your hedgie in this easier to eat format.

Hedgehog chow

In the past, foods labeled as hedgehog diets were all pretty terrible for hedgehogs and owners were advised not to even consider these as options. In recent years, more high-quality hedgehog foods have started showing up in pet stores. Some good brands include Spike's Delight, Exotic Nutrition's Hedgehog Complete formula, 8in1 Ultra Hedgehog mix, and Sunseed hedgehog food. Though this isn't a complete list, you should check the label of any other brand of hedgehog chow to make sure the first two ingredients are meat or meat meal and that it contains no seeds, nuts, or raisins.

Wet dog and cat food

Canned, wet dog and cat foods should only be given to hedgehogs as treats. Make sure they're meat or poultry based and limit the amount to one teaspoon a day. Canned foods will often alter the consistency of the hedgehog's waste; it may be moist or slimy, or have a stronger odor than usual.

Live food

As insectivores in the wild, hedgehogs will appreciate the inclusion of live food in their diet. This should be a supplement to dry kibble—a hedgehog in captivity will get too much fat and not enough other vitamins subsisting exclusively on live food. You can give them 3-5 mealworms in a day, 1-2 crickets, or a single waxworm. Insects should be gut-loaded for at least 24 hours before feeding them to your hedgehog (if you're not familiar with this term, gut-loading is a process by which an insect's nutritional value is enhanced by feeding them high-quality food).

Mealworms often come in a gut-load mix of flour and sawdust and can be left in that container. These little worms are the larval stage of the mealworm beetle. If left in a room-temperature environment, the mealworms will pupate into their adult form, a medium-sized black beetle that can also be fed to the hedgehog, or left in the container to lay eggs and form a self-sustaining colony. If you'd rather not deal with beetles, you can prevent pupation by keeping the mealworms in the fridge. Don't feed freeze dried mealworms to your hedgehog—these have been implicated in instances of impacted bowels.

Crickets should be kept in a plastic container with a tight-sealing lid. You can find cricket gut-load formula in the reptile section of the pet store. Provide the crickets with a slice of a hard fruit or vegetable for water (like a melon, potato, apple, or pear). Crickets are more difficult to breed, and considering how few you'll need for your hedgehog, you'll likely be best served by buying only as much as you need for a few feedings from your local pet store.

Fruits and vegetables

Fruits and vegetables should be considered treats for a hedgehog. Give them only small amounts per day (less than a teaspoon). Avoid avocado and grapes, as mentioned above; otherwise, all fruits and vegetables are fair game. Food enjoyed by most hedgehogs include peas, corn, yams, apples, melon, and bananas.

Cooked meats

Some other human food can be an appropriate treat for a hedgie. Poultry and hamburger are popular hedgehog treats. Make sure the meat is unseasoned and avoid pre-packaged lunch meats or other items containing lots of salt and preservatives. As with the other treats above, offer them no more than 1 teaspoon in any given day.

Supplements

If your hedgehog has dry skin issues you can add a few drops of an omega fatty acid or some flax seed into their food mix. Most hedgehogs will not need other nutritional supplements. You should only give them vitamin mixes if it's recommended by your vet; due to the vitamins and minerals already present in their food, hedgehogs who are given generic small animal multi vitamins could receive too much of certain things, some of which can be accumulated in the blood to toxic levels.

Care of your hedgehog

Hedgehogs are comparatively low-maintenance animals. While they can adapt to owners with irregular days, they do best on a consistent schedule, especially with regards to light and feeding. Your daily care routine should start with a thorough inspection of the hedgehog's cage. Scoop any waste out of the litter box and wipe any visible mess off of cage walls and furnishings. Next, tend to his food. Check the dry food; if it's soiled, you should throw away any leftover dry food, but if it's clean you can keep it in the dish and refill it to the appropriate level. Give your hedgehog any wet food you want to offer him (or you can give him treats at playtime, if you'd prefer). Re-fill the water, and if it's in a bottle, check the tip to make sure there's liquid coming out. If you're using a cage liner, change it if there's any visible waste or other messes. Other beddings should be spot-cleaned.

Weekly tasks

You should thoroughly clean the hedgehog's cage once a week. Unless something's especially filthy, soap and water should work fine. Items that need a thorough disinfecting can be washed in a 10% bleach solution, then rinsed until no smell of bleach remains on the item. Remove all the furnishings from the cage and wash them. This includes the hide box, exercise wheel, and food and water dishes. If you're using a water bottle, empty it completely and wash it inside and out. Mold and algae can grow in a poorly-maintained water bottle, which could make your hedgehog sick or taint the taste of the water and make them not want to drink. If you use cage liners, make sure they get washed. You should also empty the litter box, wash it, and re-fill it with fresh litter once a week.

Monthly tasks

If you're using disposable bedding, it should be fully replaced once a month. Most people find it easiest to remember when they clean the cage if they set up some kind of consistent schedule (e.g. bedding is replaced during a month's first weekly cleaning). You should also weigh your hedgehog once a month and record that information in a ledger so you can keep track of changes. Again, most people find it easiest to do this on the same day as bedding is replaced.

You'll also want to give your hedgehog a bath about once a month (unless your pet is especially messy, in which case you'll want to do it every couple of weeks). You can bathe your hedgehog in the bathroom sink or bathtub. Some keepers like using the kitchen sink if it's got a spray attachment; if you do this, you should buy a secondary container (like a plastic dish tub) to bathe the hedgehog in, and disinfect the sink thoroughly with bleach after the bath.

To bathe your hedgehog, you'll need cat shampoo, a cup (or spray attachment), and a toothbrush. You'll also want to have a towel standing by to dry him off with when he's done. Fill the sink or tub with one inch of warm water and mix in a couple drops of cat shampoo. Thoroughly wet the hog using the cup or the sprayer, then gently scrub his quills with the toothbrush, starting at the back and working toward the front. Be careful not to get any soapy water in his eyes. To wash his belly, reach underneath him and gently massage the fur with your fingers. Do to the same to his legs and paws. Don't flip the hedgehog over! This will freak him out and he might ball up or thrash around, getting soapy water in his face and generally stressing him out. Once he's been scrubbed, take the hedgehog out of the sink or tub and drain it then refill it with another inch of clean, warm water and rinse the hog. When that's done, you can gently towel him dry. Make sure the hedgehog's completely dry before returning him to his enclosure.

You should also check your hedgehog's toenails while you're bathing him. A hedgehog's nails should not curl back under his paws; if they do, it's time for a trim. If he's got hard materials to walk on they might never need trimmed, or you might only need to get certain nails. Each nail has a small pink line running down its center. This is the quick, and it will hurt and bleed if you cut it. The clear white part of the nail is completely nerveless and if you're careful not to hit the quick, trimming the nails will cause the hedgehog no pain. Use a pair of cat claw trimmers and take off just a little at a time. Hedgehogs can get antsy during the trimming process and if he starts to squirm let him take a break or you risk injury—either to him with the clippers, or to your finger when he gets fed up and bites you. If you have to trim more than a couple nails, you'll probably have to do it over a couple days. If you do hit the quick, don't panic. Apply some styptic powder (or other absorbent powder, like corn starch or flour) to the wound until it stops bleeding, then rinse and dry the nail and keep an eye out for infection. If you're hesitant to trim the nails yourself, a vet can do it for you.

Training and discipline

When we talk about training a hedgehog, it's in a different sense than, say, training a dog. You can think of hedgehogs more as you would a neighborhood cat. It will recognize you as a source of food and care and you can form a very affectionate bond, but you shouldn't expect it to perform tricks on demand or come to you each time you call. You're not teaching the animal; more, you're suggesting an activity that is amenable to both you and the hedgie, and if it chooses to it will perform this task in exchange for some reward. You can see this in the litter training advice from the previous chapter. The hedgehog's reward for using the litter box is a clean environment. Since this is something most hedgehogs seek, they take readily to the training. Working with the hedgehog's instincts will yield the best results. Be patient with the animal, giving them some time to chill out if they show frustration by hissing or raising quills.

Reward works much better than punishment when it comes to training or disciplining a hedgehog. If you strike or yell at a hedgehog, it will only make them view you as a threat. They'll be wary of your presence and less likely to be social in general. If you're training your pet to run a maze, put a treat at the end to entice him. If you're socializing him to new people, offer treats for major milestones, like the first time he relaxes in a stranger's lap. The deterrent methods listed earlier for dealing with habitual biting are the main exception to this, and even in that case should be paired with a reward to reinforce good behavior, such as a treat following a play session with no biting incidents.

Daily play and exercise

Now to the fun part of hedgehog care: Playtime! If you get your hedgehog on a regular schedule, you'll likely find him waiting for you at the cage door when playtime comes around. The nature of your play is going to depend a lot on the interests and personality of your particular animal, but in every case variety is key. Hedgehogs are intelligent and inquisitive animals that enjoy exploring new things.

You've got a lot of play area options to work with. You could use any of the playpen options mentioned in chapter 2, but if you'd rather not buy an external structure—or if you have limited space—several areas of your home can be easily adapted. The simplest option is a standard bathtub. The sides are too tall and smooth for a hedgehog to climb up and out, so you don't need to take any extra security measures aside from making sure the drain is firmly stoppered. You can use a pet gate or baby gate to close off a closet or other section of a room. If you can, find a gate with ½ inch or smaller gaps between the bars; if that's not available, buy a sheet of smooth metal or plastic to cover it and prevent escape. Some owners will let their hedgehogs out to explore and play in an entire room, or even their entire apartment—in fact, free-roaming hedgehogs are not unheard of.

Any area that's going to serve as a play space needs to be hedgie-proofed for safety. Hedgehogs aren't known to chew on non-food items the way rodents do, though they will eat something if they think it's food, and they will often lick strong-smelling items, either to determine edibility or to self-anoint with the odor. You should make sure nothing is accessible in the hedgehog's play area that could be toxic if licked or eaten. The other behaviors you have to worry about during playtime are climbing and burrowing. Hedgehogs are accomplished climbers, but they aren't always as good at getting back down. If you're letting your hedgehog roam in a whole house or room, make sure he can't climb his way into any dangerous situations. Since they burrow, you also have to be careful of gaps in walls and cabinetry. You should also make sure they can't get under, inside, or behind any appliances (refrigerators, washing machines, etc) where they could get stuck, lost, or injured. Radiators and heating vents should also be covered or blocked off. Finally, you need to make sure there's no way for the hedgehog to get outside through a window, doggie door, or other opening. Once they're in the open, hedgehogs run surprisingly fast, and they could be gone before you have a chance to react.

Outdoor play

It can be fun to take your hedgehog outside for some fresh air, so long as you follow some basic safety precautions. First of all, make sure the air temperature is within the acceptable range of 70°-90°F (and make sure to factor any kind of wind into that equation). You'll mostly want to take them outside in the evening when they'd normally be awake. This will keep them from getting overheated by direct sunlight. It's also not a good idea to take a hedgehog outside when it's raining. They like a drier environment, and they'll get cold if they get wet.

Any time your hedgehog is outside they should be in a secure, supervised area. You can use a rabbit hutch or move their playpen or cage outside. Whatever space you provide should include both shade and water. Remember that they burrow; the grass in your yard is not necessarily a secure barrier, and whatever insects or worms they happen upon while digging will probably be eaten. If you don't want to worry about them digging, put a layer of something solid between the hedgehog and the grass. You could use a blanket, a sheet of pressed wood or acrylic, a canvas tarp—pretty much anything that's non-toxic and can't be burrowed through.

Be aware of all potential environmental hazards before you take your pet outside. Don't put them on a lawn that's been chemically treated. If your neighborhood has a lot of free-roaming cats (or other predators) a covered enclosure is necessary. The space should also be clean of other animals' waste. Raccoon droppings can be especially bad for hedgehogs. Raccoon roundworm (*Baylisascaris procyonis*) is a parasite that's transmitted through physical contact and can be contracted by hedgehogs. The eggs of this parasite can stay alive in the soil for years, so be especially cautious letting your pet burrow in areas where raccoons are common.

Toys

Most hedgehogs can learn how to run a maze in search of treats. You can build them one using blocks or set up a system of tunnels out of the plastic pieces they sell in the small animal section—just be sure to buy the ferret size; hedgehogs can get stuck in tubes designed for hamsters and gerbils. Aside from these products, most toys aimed at small animals aren't the best for hedgehogs. Unlike other rodents, they don't need to chew on wood to file down their teeth, and a lot of the toys designed for hamsters and gerbils are choking hazards if given to a hedgehog. You also shouldn't use the clear plastic hamster balls or runaround balls. Since hedgehogs like to poop while they're running these will get your pet pretty messy, and the ventilation slits in these products are also known to catch quills and toes.

If you want to get toys at the pet store, look for them in the cat and dog sections. Both balls and squeak toys usually appeal to hedgehogs. The general consensus among breeders is that you shouldn't give hedgehogs straight catnip, but cat toys with catnip inside won't harm a hedgehog—they're not generally known for destroying toys and will be unlikely to eat any. The only cat toys you should avoid are the slitted hard plastic balls, as the hedgehog's teeth and toes can get stuck in the gaps. From the dog section, balls and squeaky toys are both good options.

You can also use children's toys and stuffed animals. Hedgehogs seem to greatly enjoy pushing toy cars around their playpen, and you can have some fun with kids' construction toys (dumptrucks, backhoes, etc) by putting treats in the compartment and watching your hedgehog learn how to get to them. Online hedgehog forums are full of wonderful ideas for playthings. Even something as simple as a disposable paper bowl can be an engaging addition to a playpen. Just make sure anything you offer follows the same rules as the bedding and cage: it should be non-toxic, contain no cedar, pine, lead, or zinc, and have no stray threads or sharp edges.

Chapter 4: Health and wellness

Provided they receive proper food and housing, hedgehogs are not susceptible to many illnesses or sensitive to toxins during the first five or so years of their life. Older hedgehogs, unfortunately, are prone to many cancers, and this is the primary cause of health complications in elderly hogs. Some of the most common health issues—like dry skin and obesity—may not require veterinary attention, provided you monitor your pet's health closely enough to catch the issue early.

Like many small animals, hedgehogs have evolved not to show illness or injury readily. In the wild, this is a matter of survival—sick, weak animals are often the first to be taken by predators. In captivity, this can make it difficult to tell something's wrong until it's too late. Fortunately, there are some signs of a problem that a keen pet owner will be able to notice. It's not normal for a hedgehog to scratch or gnaw on itself frequently. If it's doing this, it at the least has dry skin, and may have an external parasite or allergic reaction to something in its cage. A hedgehog's ears should have smooth edges. If they're ragged or have finger-like protrusions, he's probably got some kind of ear infection or fungal growth. Persistently runny, smelly, or odd-colored stool is usually an indication of an internal parasite or infection. Discharge from the eyes, ears, or nose is a sign of infection. Other signs include sluggishness, lack of appetite, sudden weight changes, lumps or sores on the skin, excessive quill loss, cloudy eyes, or changes in water consumption are other good signs that something's wrong. If you notice any of these things, you should immediately make an appointment with your vet.

Visits to the vet

Since hedgehogs are still considered exotic pets, it can be difficult to find a vet who's willing to treat them and knowledgeable enough to be of use. Exotic pet veterinarians are getting more common, and if you live in a city you'll probably be able to find at least one. More rural owners, though, may need to drive a significant distance. You should find the closest vet and make an appointment for an initial check-up as soon as possible after getting the animal home so you don't have to scramble if there is a problem down the line. Yearly check-ups are also a good idea; you may want to increase that to twice a year visits for hedgehogs over the age of five. If you're not sure how to find a vet in your area, the Hedgehog Welfare Society has compiled a fairly comprehensive list at their website (www.hedgehogwelfare.org/veterinarians.asp). You should expect the bill to be at least $50 for a hedgehog's vet visit, and it could range up into the thousands if surgery or serious medication is required.

Getting your hedgehog to a vet can also be a bit of an ordeal. If your cage is large, heavy, or unwieldy, you'll want to buy a small, secure container to transport him in. A cat carrier will work well, or a plastic habitat or glass aquarium. Make sure whatever container you're using has good ventilation. If it's winter, warm up the car before bringing your animal out and put some kind of heating device—like hand warmers or a heating pad on the lowest setting, wrapped in a towel—inside the carrier to keep the hedgehog warm. Sudden chill is bad even for a healthy hedgehog, and could prove fatal for one that's already sick. If it's summer, make sure to keep the carrier out of direct sunlight and don't put it directly in front of any air conditioning vents. A few scraps of cloth or bedding for the hedgehog to nestle with inside the carrier can't hurt either.

Quilling

If your hedgehog is an adult it should never lose more than a few quills at a time (if he does, that's a sign of a skin infection and he should be taken to the vet) but a growing hedgehog goes through four quillings during its adolescence. The first occurs at about 4 weeks; the final (adult) quilling usually occurs around 12 weeks. A quilling can last anywhere from 2-6 weeks and can be viewed as your hedgehog's version of teething (or, alternatively, his "terrible twos"). He will be very grumpy and will not want to be touched during the process—which is understandable; you probably wouldn't want someone touching you, either, if you had thousands of needles pushing through your skin. For the most part, you just have to ride out the quilling and trust that your hedgehog's personality will return to normal once the process is over. If you want to help him along you can give him a bath in lukewarm water with a capful of olive oil mixed in. This should soften the skin and help reduce the pain of the new quills coming in. Don't towel dry him afterwards; instead, use a hair drier on its lowest setting.

Hibernation and aestivation

Hibernation can be fatal for captive hedgehogs because they're not supposed to be doing it— hibernation is a common thing for European hedgehogs, but not for those of African origin. Since they don't have to cope with cold winters, African hedgehogs have un-learned the hibernating behavior to some extent and their metabolisms don't slow enough when they enter the torpor state. Captive hedgehogs who hibernate may die of starvation or hypothermia. Hibernation can be triggered both by temperatures that are too cold and by sudden drops in temperature, even within the recommended range. It can also be triggered by inconsistencies in the day/night cycle and is another reason you should always maintain a consistent photoperiod. A hedgehog that enters hibernation is unlikely to recover if not revived after the first 72 hours, so if you notice it's happening, you should act quickly.

If your hedgehog refuses to eat and drink and is acting especially sluggish or depressed, he may be entering hibernation. Check the hedgie's stomach. If it's cold, you need to warm him up immediately. Put the hedgehog against your chest under a blanket or sweater. Speak to it in soft, soothing tones and stay calm—it will pick up on your emotional state. You could also wrap it in towels fresh from the drier. While you're warming him, make sure the cage is at least 74°F and raise the temperature, if necessary. Don't put the hedgehog in hot water or directly in front of a heater. That can raise his temperature too quickly. With the slow warming from your body heat, the hedgehog should revive and resume a normal activity level within 10-15 minutes. If he doesn't, you should call a vet immediately.

Aestivation is the hedgehog's response to the other end of the spectrum—an environment that's too hot. This is much more common and less harmful for

African hedgehogs, though it still is a sign you need to tweak the enclosure. A hedgehog that's too hot will lay flat on its belly with its legs spread out and will start to pant. If you notice your hedgehog doing this, lower the temperature inside its cage. This could mean turning up the air conditioning, or putting bowls of ice on the top of the cage—the cool air should drift down and perk the hedgehog right up. Like with hibernation above, don't put fans directly on him or run him under cold water. This will lower his temperature too quickly and could cause further complications.

Parasites and fungus

This is the most common health affliction for hedgehogs of all ages. Fungus growth is especially common on the ears. This can take the form of rough or dry edges, or of finger-like growths outwards from the ears. This last ailment is a fungus commonly found in wood products and actually eats away at the skin of the ears. If you notice this, take the animal to the vet as soon as possible.

Mites are the most common external parasite for hedgehogs. These look like tiny white dots, about the size of the head of a pin. You may be able to see them moving on your hedgehog, or you might notice him scratching and biting at himself. A vet can give you a topical medication to get rid of the mites. Hedgehogs that share their space with other animals—or who go outside a lot—are also likely to pick up fleas. You can usually get rid of them with a bath in flea shampoo, but check the ingredients first and make sure you don't use any product containing Ivermectin, which has been implicated in the deaths of some captive hedgehogs. Hedgehogs can also pick up ticks. If you notice one on your hedgehog, don't pull it out immediately—the mouth parts can get left behind in the skin and lead to infection. Coat the tick's body with petroleum jelly until it stops moving, then remove it with tweezers and disinfect the area. If your hedgehog is afflicted by any external parasite, you should clean and disinfect the cage and all its furnishings, and throw away any furnishings or bedding made of wood, paper, or other porous materials, as these may be harboring eggs and could cause a re-infestation.

Internal parasites are harder to diagnose, and can mostly be identified by looking at the hedgehog's poop, which will be runny, smelly, or green. These can usually be removed easily with oral medication prescribed by your veterinarian. Like with fleas and mites, you should clean and disinfect the entire cage of a hedgehog suffering from internal parasites.

Dry skin

If your hedgehog has no parasites but is still scratching, has flaky or red skin, or is losing an unusual amount of quills, he's probably got dry skin. This tends to be more of a problem in the winter. You can apply a couple drops of vitamin E directly to his back or rump, or add a small amount of cod liver oil or a supplement containing omega fatty acids to his diet. Just make sure to monitor his weight while he's receiving oral oils so he doesn't become obese.

Gastro-intestinal issues

If your hedgehog has diarrhea or is vomiting, he may have a stomach bug. Remove all his food and offer him small amounts of water. Clean and disinfect all of his food containers and save a bit of stool for the vet to examine. You should be especially careful of dehydration in a pet with these issues. Lift up a small amount of the skin on his back, then let it go. It should return to normal right away; if it doesn't, the animal is dehydrated. Offer your hedgehog some warmed pediatric electrolyte solution (this can be found in the baby food section of the grocery store) with an oral syringe or eye dropper. If he throws this up, seek medical help immediately.

Constipation can also be an issue for hedgehogs, usually caused by changes in their diet. If your hedgehog's constipated, you can put him in a couple inches of warm water, or feed him a spoonful of unseasoned canned pumpkin. If neither of these things work, his bowels may be impacted and you should call your vet.

Obesity

A normal-weight hedgehog should have a "leggy" appearance when it's running. The stomach should not drag on the floor, and there should be no rolls under his arms or chin. An obese hedgehog will be sluggish and cranky, and may even have difficulty rolling himself into a ball. Obesity causes a wide range of health issues in hedgehogs, from kidney and liver failure to heart and respiratory issues. If your hedgehog is obese, remove all wet food and treats from his diet and switch him to a low-calorie kibble formula, if he's not on one already. Also make sure the pet is getting enough exercise. You may need to increase his daily play time. Also make sure there are no issues with his wheel that are preventing him from using it.

Tooth disease

Hedgehogs that don't get enough hard food to stimulate their gum tissue are prone to tooth loss and gum disease. A normal hedgie mouth has white teeth and pink gums. If the gums are red or swollen, the teeth are discolored, or the animal's pawing at his mouth, he may have an infection and you should take him to the vet just to be sure. Other signs of tooth disease include loss of appetite, drooling, and foul breath.

Older hedgehog ailments

As hedgehogs age, they're prone to developing more health issues, the most serious of which is cancer. This can affect every organ of the body, and can be treated with chemotherapy or surgery. Signs of cancer include unusual lumps under the skin, or the other signs of illness like sluggishness and appetite loss.

Older hedgehogs also frequently suffer kidney issues. This can be identified by sudden weight loss, lethargy, anemia, and changes in the waste. Oral diseases are also more common in older hedgehogs.

There's no surefire way to prevent any of these illnesses, but keeping the cage a little warmer for a hedgehog over the age of five—around 80°F—can help keep them healthier longer.

Other issues

Hedgehogs kept in an environment that's too cool or too moist are prone to developing respiratory diseases. Signs of this are similar to a human's common cold—sneezing, nasal discharge, difficulty breathing, or wheezing sounds while breathing. Give the enclosure a good thorough cleaning and raise the temperature a few degrees. If the symptoms don't improve within a week, call your vet.

Hedgehogs carry salmonella but very rarely will contract it. If they do, you'll notice flu-like symptoms and will need to call your vet. Similarly rare conditions include urinary tract infections, eye infections, and shock from an invisible injury. The best bet in all of these cases is to get medical help rather than trying to treat the issue yourself.

Finally, the hedgehog's quills can make it difficult to properly cover small wounds to keep them from getting infected. If your hedgehog gets small cuts that don't bleed too much you can affix a piece of gauze over the wound and hold it in place with a solid strip of sock material. Slide it over the front of the hedgehog; it should hold the gauze tight to the body. If there's profuse bleeding—or if the hedgehog is bleeding from the nose or mouth after a fall or injury—you should seek medical attention.

Administering medicine

Since your hedgehog is already sick, you should try to make the administration of medications as low-stress as possible. If you're putting topical medication on a wound or skin infection, don't apply too much. If the hedgehog thinks it smells or tastes good it can re-open the wound by repeatedly licking or chewing on the area. You may need to get a plastic shield of the same style given to dogs and cats post-surgery from your vet if they refuse to stop licking the area.

When you're administering medicine orally, try to make it part of a treat as often as possible. Hedgehogs have a sweet tooth so mix it with some mushed-up fruit or use some natural flavoring from the baking section to give it a pleasant odor and flavor. You can also mix the medication with human baby foods based on strained meats, like chicken and turkey, or with their wet dog or cat food. Don't mix the medication into an entire bowl of dry food as you won't be sure that the hedgehog will eat the whole dose.

Hedgehogs are fairly tolerant of injectable medications, though they may pop and jump the first time you try it. You can give an injectable medication even if the hedgehog's in a ball; have your vet show you the ideal way to administer that particular injection.

The hardest medications to give to a hedgehog are those that have to go directly into the ears or eye. Your best bet for getting these into your hedgehog is to use a scruff hold. This is the way mother hedgehogs carry their young in the wild, so while it might look painful a scruff hold will actually help relax them. Put on a pair of latex gloves to get better traction on the quills and gently grab the hedgehog slightly behind his ears, lifting him until his rear legs are suspended. Once he's relaxed his mouth should be slack and his eyes almost closed. At this point, you can use an eye dropper to administer the medication. Make sure the medication is at room temperature to limit discomfort, and try not to touch his sensitive face hairs or it may cause him to break out of his relaxed

trance.

Chapter 5: Breeding and showing

Some keepers who want to take their love of hedgehogs to the next level will either breed them or show them. Either one of these things can be a very time consuming hobby and you should think carefully about your own schedule and the health and personality of your pet before deciding to move forward, though in both cases the end results can be very rewarding.

Hedgehog shows

The first hedgehog show was held in 1995 in Tacoma, Washington. In the two decades since, nearly 100 shows have been held across North America. These shows are similar to dog shows, where the individuals are judged on the basis of temperament and appearance. If you are interested in showing your hedgehog, you can find out more in-depth information or register your animal with the International Hedgehog Association (www.hedgehogclub.com/shows.html). The website isn't especially great about updating its "upcoming shows" section, so you'll probably find it easier to ask around in forums or Google search to find the events that are coming up in your area.

When hedgehogs are shown, they're judged on a point system in a variety of categories. The largest number of points (33 possible) come from temperament. Judges are looking for a calm animal that's unrolled and has its quills flat. They also give points for personality, and deduct 22 points (or all points for temperament, if they didn't reach 22) if the hedgehog bites. The next biggest point section is for the animal's form (25 possible) with points for the animal's healthy weight and profile, as well as the shape of the rump and the flow of movement. The rest of the points are given based on appearance, with sections for the color and patterning, the quills, the legs, the ears, and the face. It's important to note that even the most beautifully perfect-looking hedgehog won't do well at a show if it's not pleasant when around people.

In addition to awarding prizes for animals that excel, hedgehog shows serve as a meeting point for breeders and owners across the nation and can be a great place to get up to date on the latest in hedgehog care and knowledge. The goal of these shows is to disseminate as much knowledge as possible about the proper care and handling of these unique and beautiful animals. Even if you don't plan on showing your hedgehogs, it may be worth it to check out a show in your area if you find yourself getting into the culture of hedgehog ownership.

Entering a show

The group sponsoring each show will have entry forms available. Most shows will let you enter an animal up through the day of the show, but this is usually more expensive than pre-registering and you should check on the guidelines of the individual event to be sure. Hedgehogs are first broken down by color class, then by age: Hedgehogs between 3 and 11 months are "A" class, and those older than 11 months are "B" class. Remember this is the age of the hedgehog at the time of the show. Color classes are discussed in more detail below. You can leave this section blank if you're not sure where your animal fits; the judge can decide when you arrive.

Attendance at these shows usually costs between $20 and $100. Registering animals for judging or to participate in obstacle courses, games, and other events is usually cheaper—$5-$20 per animal (though you'll need to buy an attendance pass before you can register your pet).

Preparing for a show

The maximum cage size at a hedgehog show is 2'X3', so you will likely need to buy a special enclosure for show days. Make sure your animal has a bath and a nail trim a day or so before the show—you want him to put his best paw forward! If your animal develops any illnesses or contracts a parasite in the days before the show, you should not take him to the event. Not only could the movement stress out your animal and make him sicker, whatever he has might be contagious and could spread to other animals at the event.

Show classes

There are 7 color classes recognized by the IHA. Including variants within the classes, there are a total of 92 recognized colorations. The 7 official classes are:

Pinto—Pinto is a patterning more than a coloration, and is the name given to any animal with patches of quill and skin that lack color, typically in a circular spot on either side. Pinto animals are judged on the symmetry of the patterning as well as the overall appearance.

Standard Coat—This is a hedgehog's "normal" color pattern, with the black-banded white quills often referred to as either "salt and pepper" or "agouti." This category also includes chocolate (dark brown) and gray or dark gray colorations.

Apricot—This category also includes, cinnamon, cinnacot, and champagne colorations—pretty much anything that's more orangey than brown or black. All of these tend toward a pale orange-beige in the banding of the quills, and the animals may feature dark or ruby red eyes.

Snowflake—Snowflake animals have a mix of banded and non-banded quills, giving them a "snow dusted" look. The base color could be from any of the color categories, so long as about 50% of the quills are unbanded. The category also includes silver and charcoal variants.

White—Hedgehogs in the white category have no bands on the quills on their body, though they may have banded quills on the forehead. This is different from albino animals in that the skin, nose, and eyes retain pigmentation.

Albino—Albino animals have absolutely no pigmentation, giving them a pink nose and red eyes as well as a pure white coat.

Any other color—This is the catch-all category for colorations that don't fit into the others. Included in this category are double-white, confetti, and tri varieties.

Breeding hedgehogs

Breeding hedgehogs is not easy. Getting them to mate is no problem—if you house a male and female together they'll do it whether or not you intend them to—but ensuring a healthy delivery and keeping newborn hoglets alive requires constant attention and care. It's even difficult to tell when a female hedgehog is pregnant. You should also be aware from the start that not all of the hoglets will live to adulthood. A female hedgehog can theoretically give birth to anywhere from 1-11 babies per year without sacrificing her own health, but approximately 1/3 of the hoglets from any given litter will die before they're 4 weeks old, even in ideal conditions. Complications from breeding can kill a female hedgehog. It is not recommended to start breeding your hedgehogs until you have at least two years of experience in specifically hedgehog care. If you are committed to breeding your hedgehogs, you should seek advice from outside sources—including your vet, local breeders, scientific literature, and online forums—before you begin. The information provided here is not a comprehensive guide—consider it more an introduction to the idea of breeding (or an emergency reference guide should you find yourself with one of those "teen moms" mentioned in chapter 1).

Mating your hedgehogs

Hedgehogs aren't fully mature until they're about 6 months old. Though they can become sexually active much younger than that, you should wait until at least the 6 month mark to start breeding females. Males can theoretically start breeding at 4 months, though they may not be fertile until the 5 or 6 month mark. Keep your breeding pair separate if either individual is younger than this. Hoglets born to an immature female can be stunted, stillborn, and generally sickly. An immature mother is also more likely to die of complications, or to neglect (or even eat) the young.

Even a male/female hedgehog pairing that you plan to breed should be given separate housing. Partially this is to prevent the male from over-mating the female, which he will if given the opportunity. This is also for the protection of the hoglets—hedgehog mothers will usually care for their young, but hedgehog fathers are more likely to eat them.

Hedgehogs are most likely to breed successfully from April through September. Do not take this to mean it's okay to house the genders together from October to March—this just means, if you're trying to breed, you will have the best shot of achieving pregnancy from late spring to early fall. Mating happens quickly, and the male should need no more encouragement than shared playtime with a female to mount and mate with her.

The pregnancy

As mentioned earlier, it can be very difficult to tell when your female is pregnant. About half of all copulations result in pregnancy. Hedgehog gestation lasts anywhere from 1-2 months, with an average length of around 35 days. If you've observed your hedgehogs mating, you should treat your female as if she's pregnant until two months have passed since the last breeding opportunity. This means you should not attempt to mate her again assuming the first time didn't take. It also means you should make sure she's got adequate hiding space in which to make her nest, and you should provide her with extra soft nesting material, like scraps of fleece or flannel, or recycled paper bedding.

At around the 20-day mark you should remove the wheel from the mother's cage, and keep it out until the babies are completely weaned. Running on the wheel could cause premature birth, or cause injury to the developing embryos. After birth, you run the risk of the mother ignoring the babies. Alternatively, she might try to bring her babies with her on her "journey," trampling or injuring them in the process.

If you typically use a water dish, you should replace this with a bottle at the same point that you take out the wheel. Baby hoglets have been known to drown in water dishes.

Raising the hoglets

Once there are hoglets in the nest you should disturb the mother as little as possible. You'll know the hoglets are there because you'll hear them chirping, even if you can't see them. Resist the temptation to pick up or otherwise interact with the babies. A mother whose nest is disturbed will often eat her young. For the first 10-14 days, you should do nothing except provide the mother with fresh food and water. You can scoop the litter box (quietly) but should not clean the cage or remove the mother. The only exception to this is if you notice any significant amount of blood in the cage. This is an indication of serious post-birth complications and you need to take your hedgehog to the vet immediately. You may run the risk of disturbing the nest, but if you don't you're likely to lose the babies and the mother.

Very rarely, a mother will not care for her young. In this instance, hand-rearing will be necessary. For the first three weeks, you can feed the babies goat's milk or a milk replacement with similar nutritional content. The hoglets' eyes aren't open yet, and they won't be able to search for food; you'll have to feed them by hand using an eye dropper or an oral syringe. Bottle-fed hedgehogs will also need to be manually stimulated to release waste. You can do this by stroking their rear end with a warm, damp cotton ball, or a large Q-tip. Once a hoglet's eyes are open, they'll start moving around and you can switch them to a meat-based baby food. They'll be prepared to switch to dry kitten food once they're weaned, at about 5-6 weeks. At this point, you should also separate the males from the females (including the mother) to prevent an unintended pregnancy.

Additional Resources

For additional reading, I recommend these two internet forums:

http://www.hedgehogcentral.com/forums/

http://www.hedgehogworld.com/forum.php

Made in the USA
Middletown, DE
26 May 2016